# Looking After Our World

Written by Claire Halliday

Series Consultant: Linda Hoyt

WorldWise™
Content-based Learning

# Contents

Victoria Falls, Zambia-Zimbabwe
Great Barrier Reef, Australia

# Chapter 1
# Our wonderful world

Our world is an amazing place. It has huge mountains, deep canyons, enormous waterfalls and colourful coral reefs. Some places are so amazing that people have made them world **heritage** sites. This means that they have been protected so that people now and in years to come can enjoy and learn about these sites.

Grand Canyon, USA

Places become world heritage sites for different reasons. Many world heritage sites arc natural wilderness areas that have **unique** features, such as the Grand Canyon in the United States.

The United Nations Educational, Scientific, and Cultural Organization (UNESCO) decides which places should become world heritage sites.

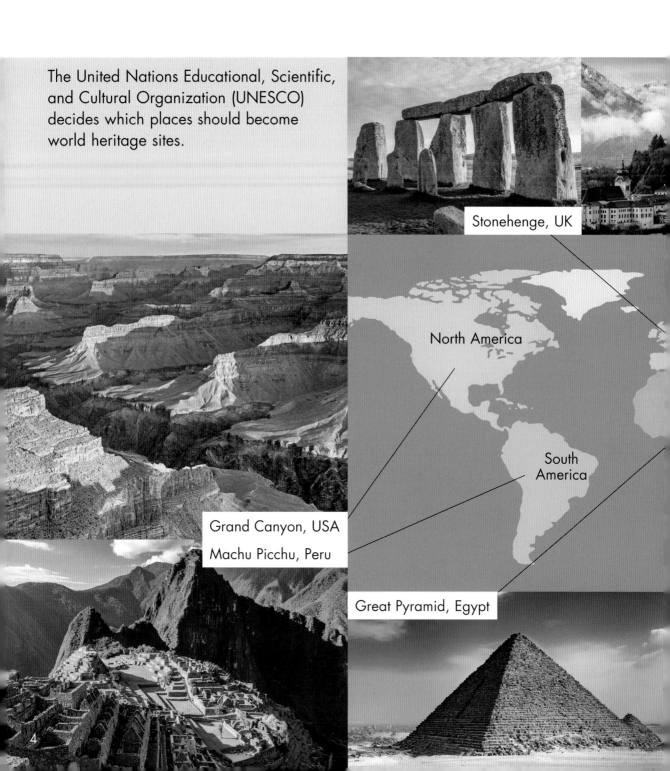

Stonehenge, UK

North America

South America

Grand Canyon, USA

Machu Picchu, Peru

Great Pyramid, Egypt

Other places have become world heritage sites because they have both cultural and natural features, such as Uluru-Kata Tjuta National Park in Australia. Some world heritage sites are amazing examples of things that people have created, such as the Great Wall in China. When UNESCO identifies a world heritage site, people must try to protect and **preserve** it for others to enjoy in the future.

Salzburg, Austria

Great Wall, China

Europe

Asia

Africa

Australia

Uluṟu–Kata Tjuṯa National Park, Australia

Tongariro National Park, New Zealand

iSimangaliso Wetland Park, South Africa

# Chapter 2

# Preserving natural heritage

## Fact file

**Location:** KwaZulu-Natal, South Africa

**Size:** 2,600 square kilometres

**Number of visitors a year:** one million approximately

iSimangaliso is isiZulu for "miracle".

Some places become world **heritage** sites because they are home to a large number of living things or they are places of great natural beauty.

## iSimangaliso Wetland Park

iSimangaliso Wetland Park, previously known as Greater Saint Lucia Wetland Park, is in South Africa. The park is an amazing and **unique** place because many thousands of species of different animals and plants live there. The park is made up of wetlands, lakes, beaches and coral reefs, as well as forests, grasslands and **savanna**. The animals and plants that live at iSimangaliso Wetland Park are protected because the park is a world heritage site.

iSimangaliso Wetland Park is home to an enormous number of different plant species and more than 500 species of birds. There is a diverse range of animals that live in the park. Some animals were thought to be almost extinct, and others are extremely rare.

## Protecting elephants

Elephants in this region were hunted to extinction 85 years ago. But people have worked hard to bring back other elephants from nearby parks to start new herds in iSimangaliso Wetland Park. At first, the elephants were put into a small pen to let them get used to their new home. Then they were freed into the wider park. Since then, the elephants have made themselves at home.

## Ancient fish

The ancient fish coelacanth has been found in a **submarine** canyon in this park. This fish, once thought to have been extinct for 65 million years, was rediscovered in 1938. But no one knew until recently that it was alive and well in iSimangaliso Wetland Park.

Animals such as bison, deer, hippopotamuses, rhinoceroses, turtles, kudu, zebras, buffalo and many different species of birds and fish make their home in iSimangaliso Wetland Park.

# Chapter 3

# Custodians of the land

## Fact file

**Location:** Northern Territory, Australia
**Size:** 3,800 square kilometres
**Number of visitors a year:** 300,000

## Did you know?

Uluru used to be called Ayers Rock. Why? Why the change?

While many world **heritage** sites are places that have amazing natural features, some sites **preserve** an important cultural link with people who lived there in the past.

## Uluru–Kata Tjuta National Park

Uluru–Kata Tjuta National Park is in the Northern Territory, Australia. There are two enormous rock formations in the park, as well as many other incredible rock formations. One enormous formation is Uluru, which is the largest single rock in the world. It is also the home of the Anangu, the group of Aboriginal Australians who have lived in the area for thousands of years. They own the land.

The Australian government and the Anangu people run the park together. In this way, the **customs** and beliefs of the Anangu people can be kept alive, while people from all around the world can visit the park. Government scientists and local people work together to preserve the land and ways of life of the Anangu people.

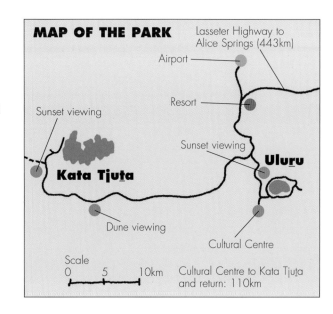

**MAP OF THE PARK**

Lasseter Highway to Alice Springs (443km)

Airport

Resort

Sunset viewing

Sunset viewing

**Uluṟu**

**Kata Tjuṯa**

Dune viewing

Cultural Centre

Scale
0        5        10km

Cultural Centre to Kata Tjuṯa and return: 110km

Uluṟu is the largest single rock in the world.

Uluṟu–Kata Tjuṯa National Park

## Park rangers

Park rangers work together to help people understand the importance of respecting and caring for the land. They teach people about Aboriginal customs and beliefs to help preserve them. Park rangers encourage people to respect the habitats of native plants and animals. Visitors should stay on the walking tracks so habitats are not harmed. People must take care of the land so that future generations of people can enjoy the park.

### Park life

As well as incredible rock formations and plant life, there are 21 species of mammals, 73 species of reptiles, 178 species of birds and 4 species of frogs in the park.

## About local people

Australian Aboriginal culture is one of the world's oldest surviving cultures and has existed for at least 50,000 years. Some groups of Aboriginal people have their own traditional lands. Aboriginal peoples' relationship with the land is the basis of their spiritual life, a tradition that is still respected today.

The Anangu people do not climb Uluru because it is **sacred** to them. They have not closed the walk, but they ask visitors to choose not to climb out of respect for their customs.

## Look out!

Here are some of the animals you might see while you are walking around Uluru–Kata Tjuta National Park. They are all able to cope with the harsh desert conditions in the park.

Blue-tongue lizard

Frill-necked lizard

Bilby

Kangaroo

Cockatoo

Dingo

# Tongariro National Park

Tongariro National Park is located on the North Island of New Zealand. It is the country's oldest National Park and is the fourth National Park to be created anywhere in the world. The park was established in 1887 and has gained international significance by being awarded UNESCO dual World Heritage. This special status recognises the park's impressive volcanic features, as well as its important cultural and spiritual connections to Maōri people.

## Fact file
**Location:**
North island of New Zealand
**Size:** 79,596 hectares
**Number of visitors a year:**
Approximately one million

## Did you know?
The 19.4 kilometre Tongariro Alpine Crossing is regarded as one of the world's best treks. Trekkers must prepare for unpredictable, rough weather and be fit and strong.

Waterfall in Tongariro National Park, New Zealand

Volcanic eruptions over the past 300,000 years, combined with glaciers from the last ice age, have formed the unique landscape of Tongariro National Park. The three major mountains in the park are all active volcanoes. Visitors can also see a wide variety of alpine plants, including some that live at high altitudes and survive very harsh conditions in snow and wind.

Blue Lake

A fantail
A grey warbler
A kereru
A brown kiwi

## What can you see in Tongariro National Park?

### Active volcanoes
Mount Ruapehu
(2,797 metres)
Mount Ngauruhoe
(2,291 metres)
Mount Tongariro
(1,968 metres)

### Birds
Around 56 different species of birds live at Tongariro. They include the tomtit, robin, tui, grey warbler, rifleman/titipounamu, bellbird/korimako, fantail/piwakawaka, and wood pigeon/kereru, and the North Island brown kiwi.

### Native mammals
New Zealand's only native mammals, short- and long-tailed bats, make their home in the Tongariro National Park.

### Some park activities
Hiking, mountain biking, paddle boarding, canoeing, rafting, fly fishing, skiing, snow boarding, bird-watching

### The important work of park rangers

The lower slopes of the mountains are covered in forest, which is an ideal home for the many different species of birds that live at Tongariro. One of the important jobs the park rangers do is oversee the kiwi sanctuary. The kiwi is a native New Zealand bird that is carefully monitored and protected.

Park rangers also spend time controlling some of the introduced wildlife that can have a negative impact on the native flora and fauna in the park. These include, black rats, stoats, cats, rabbits, hares, possums and red deer.

Although park rangers mainly help look after the plants and animals living in the region, at Tongariro National Park looking after the safety of people is also part of their role. With more than 120,000 people a year hiking the potentially dangerous Tongariro Alpine Crossing, educating visitors about how to stay safe while in the park is vital work.

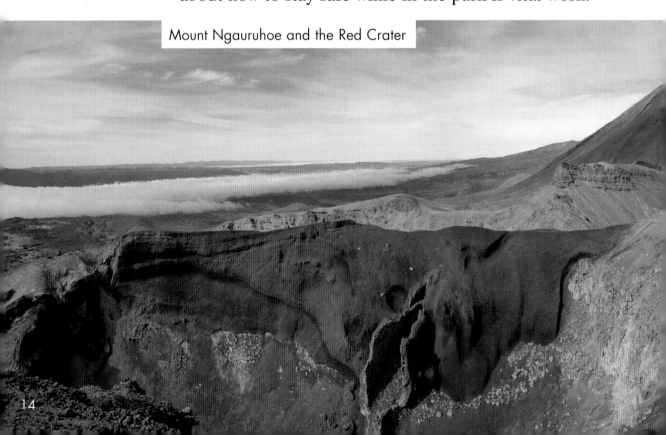

Mount Ngauruhoe and the Red Crater

## Tongariro's first people

The Tongariro region is very special to Maōri people. According to Maōri legend, the mountains at the heart of the park each have individual personalities that symbolise the links between the community and its environment.

To the local people, the three main active volcanoes, and the smaller mountains that cluster around them, were so sacred that they would not look at them directly and would not eat or build fires nearby.

Today, park rangers help educate visitors about the area's rich history to ensure it is given the respect and care it deserves for future generations to enjoy.

**Find out more**

You can become a junior ranger at a national park. Search the Internet to find out more.

Mount Ngauruhoe in winter

# Chapter 4

# Ancient monuments and cities

World **heritage** sites also include places and objects created by people, often thousands of years ago. Sites such as the Great Wall and the Mausoleum of the First Qin Emperor in China are protected because they help us to learn about how people lived long ago.

Great Wall, China

# The Mausoleum of the First Qin Emperor

In 1974, some farmers in China were digging a well when they discovered an ancient mausoleum built by the first Qin emperor. A mausoleum is a building with a tomb in it where somebody has been buried.

This mausoleum is the biggest in the world. Inside there is an army of about 8,000 life-sized **warriors** made from **terracotta**. There are also terracotta horses with the warriors, as well as bronze weapons, chariots and other **artefacts**. The mausoleum was built over 2,000 years ago. It took 700,000 workers 36 years to build the mausoleum. These workers dug large pits into which they placed the warriors standing up, and then they buried them in the tomb. The mausoleum has so much in it and is so big that it is still being excavated.

Today the mausoleum is a world heritage site, which means that it will be looked after and **preserved** into the future. People from around the world can visit the site to see this amazing ancient Chinese **monument**.

**Did you know?**

Each of the terracotta soldiers in the mausoleum has a different expression on its face.

# Salzburg, the Old City

**Think about ...**

Think about some of the older buildings in your area. Do they have any special stories? Did they ever have any special purposes?

The city of Salzburg is in Austria in Europe. Like many European cities, it has many beautiful buildings that are hundreds of years old. The centre of Salzburg is called the Old City. It has amazing buildings that show the different building styles of the past 600 years.

The people of Salzburg conserved the historical parts of the city and allowed other parts to **modernise**. In 1997, the Old City of Salzburg was made a world heritage site. Now people preserve the old city buildings and streetscapes, as well as other cultural aspects of the city's heritage, such as its music and art.

# There are many other world heritage sites in Europe.

Banks of the River Seine, including
Notre Dame, Paris, France

Vatican City, Rome, Italy

Leaning Tower, Pisa, Italy

Stonehenge, near Salisbury, England

## Historic Sanctuary of Machu Picchu

**Did you know?**

Machu Picchu is invisible from the valley below. It is often shrouded in clouds. The city is made up of palaces, baths, temples, storage rooms and houses.

The Historic Sanctuary of Machu Picchu was built over 600 years ago by the Inca people, an ancient South American civilisation. The city sits perched on a mountain top in Peru, 2,430 metres above sea level, and is very difficult to get to. It is one of the best-preserved examples of an Incan city that exists today.

One of the reasons Machu Picchu was made a world heritage site is because of how it was planned and built. The city is high up on a mountain ridge, and was built to blend into the landscape. Most of the 200 buildings in the city were made from stone blocks. The blocks were shaped so that they fitted together without using cement or mud.

The Inca people grew their food and kept livestock in and around the city. They had flowing water from a series of stone channels and **cisterns**. Their houses were built in groups of about ten and were connected by narrow alleys and shared courtyards. They also had a complex road system leading in and out of Machu Picchu.

For over 400 years, almost nobody knew anything of Machu Picchu because the Incas disappeared from the city. Machu Picchu became overgrown and was hidden from the world until it was rediscovered in 1911. People now visit the ruins of Machu Picchu. They can walk there over several days on the Inca Trail, or they can go by train.

# Preserving our heritage

World heritage sites are important natural, historical and cultural sites. They are different from each other in many ways. They are in different habitats, different climates and some can even be found in the middle of big cities.

One thing world heritage sites have in common is that they have been established to preserve and protect nature, history and culture. They aim to teach people to enjoy their heritage while protecting it.

# Glossary

**artefacts**  things created by humans

**cistern**  a tank for storing water

**customs**  practices or ways of life

**heritage**  things or places valued for their cultural, environmental or historical significance

**modernise**  to make something modern or up-to-date

**monument**  a building or statue to commemorate a special event or person

**preserve**  to stop places or things from being harmed or destroyed

**ranger**  a keeper of a park, forest or part of the countryside

**sacred**  extremely precious

**savanna**  an area of grassland with scattered trees

**submarine**  underwater

**terracotta**  brownish-red clay

**unique**  one of a kind

**warriors**  people who go to war

# Index